The Bill of Rights

The Bill of Rights:
Liberty Defined by Abuse Remembered

I0186548

**This volume is a companion to the author's five-volume
work on power, restraint, and consolidation.**

Published by Green Dragon Press
United States of America

TABLE OF CONTENTS

PREFACE

A Companion to the Five Volumes on Power and Liberty

This work was not written in isolation.

The five volumes that precede it traced a long pattern: the rise of authority, the erosion of restraint, the consolidation of power, and the recurring belief that control can be exercised safely when intentions are good. Those volumes examined cycles - how liberty fails not only through conquest, but through compliance; not only through ambition, but through demand.

The Bill of Rights occupies a unique place within that larger narrative.

Where the earlier volumes explored what happens when power expands and restraint weakens, this book examines why certain restraints were written down at all. The Bill of Rights is not an abstract philosophy of freedom. It is a catalog of historical memory. Each amendment corresponds to a failure already observed, a boundary drawn after experience removed illusion.

In the earlier volumes, power was shown to consolidate quietly. Responsibility faded. Participation declined. Institutions compensated. Authority expanded. Each step appeared justified. Each step was familiar. What changed was not human nature, but context and language.

The Bill of Rights was written by men who recognized that pattern early.

They did not assume virtue would endure. They did not trust structure alone. They believed that memory - encoded in limitation - might restrain what goodwill could not. The amendments were not written to perfect governance, but to slow its worst tendencies.

This book does not reinterpret the Bill of Rights through modern debate. It restores the historical pressure that produced it. It treats each amendment as a reaction rather than an aspiration, a denial rather than a promise.

Read alongside the earlier five volumes, this work functions as an anchor. It explains why restraint was considered necessary long before erosion and

The Bill of Rights

consolidation became visible again. It reminds the reader that what feels theoretical today was once lived experience.

Liberty was not protected because power was feared.
Power was restrained because it was understood.

INTRODUCTION

Rights Are Written After They Are Violated

The Bill of Rights was not written to expand freedom. It was written to prevent specific abuses that history had already shown were inevitable.

This distinction matters. Freedom, in the abstract, had been discussed for centuries. Philosophers debated it. Clergy preached it. Kings invoked it when convenient. Yet none of that debate prevented abuse. Liberty failed not because it was unknown, but because it was assumed. The Bill of Rights exists because assumption proved insufficient.

By the time of the American founding, the problem was no longer theoretical. English history, colonial experience, and early revolutionary governance had already revealed a consistent pattern: power expands to meet opportunity, and authority justifies itself after the fact. The abuses that followed were rarely framed as tyranny. They were presented as necessity, efficiency, order, or moral duty. Each time restraint weakened, control followed.

The framers did not believe they were inventing a new understanding of human nature. On the contrary, they believed human nature was already well understood. Ambition did not disappear when men were elected rather than crowned. Fear did not vanish when governments claimed to act in the public interest. Virtue could be sincere and still dangerous when paired with unchecked authority.

For this reason, the Constitution was designed first as a structure - a system of divided powers, competing interests, and procedural friction. But structure alone was not enough. Even a well-designed system could drift. Even elected governments could abuse. Even law itself could become an instrument of coercion.

The Bill of Rights was the corrective to that realization.

The Bill of Rights

These amendments were not aspirational poetry. They were boundaries drawn from experience. Each one corresponds to a practice already known to be destructive: compelled belief, disarmament, military intrusion, arbitrary search, forced confession, secret trials, administrative justice, excessive punishment, enumerated control, and consolidated power. None were hypothetical dangers. All had precedent.

This is why the language is restrictive rather than generous. The amendments do not say what government should do. They say what government shall not do. They do not define ideal outcomes. They deny specific authorities. The emphasis is not on trust, but on restraint.

It is also why the Bill of Rights was controversial. Some believed listing rights was unnecessary. Others feared that enumeration would invite limitation - that rights not written down might be treated as nonexistent. Both concerns were valid, and both are addressed within the document itself. The Bill of Rights is not an exhaustive catalog of liberty. It is a warning system built from memory.

Modern readers often reverse this logic. Rights are treated as abstract moral claims, detached from the abuses that necessitated them. When the original danger fades from view, the right itself begins to feel excessive, outdated, or obstructive. Enforcement becomes selective. Exceptions multiply. Language shifts. What once restrained power is recast as a problem to be managed.

This work proceeds from a different premise.

Each chapter examines one amendment not as a modern debate, but as a historical response. The focus is not on what the right promises, but on what it prevents. Not how it should evolve, but why it was written at all. Where necessary, individual clauses within an amendment will be examined separately, because many of these protections were designed to address more than one abuse at once.

The intent is not to argue policy or predict outcomes. It is to restore memory. Rights erode most quickly when their origins are forgotten. Power consolidates most easily when restraint is treated as tradition rather than necessity.

The Bill of Rights

The Bill of Rights does not assume virtue. It assumes inevitability. That assumption is the source of its strength - and the reason it still matters.

The Bill of Rights

CHAPTER 1 – The First Amendment

THE FIRST AMENDMENT
Preventing Compelled Belief and Managed Thought

This amendment addresses the most efficient form of control ever devised: the management of belief, expression, and association. It exists because history showed that authority, left unchecked, will regulate thought long before it regulates conduct.

The Text of the Amendment
Congress shall make no law respecting an establishment of religion, or prohibiting the free exercise thereof; or abridging the freedom of speech, or of the press; or the right of the people peaceably to assemble, and to petition the Government for a redress of grievances.

The Abuse That Preceded It
The First Amendment responds to a long and well-documented pattern of control exercised through belief, expression, and association.

In England, religious establishment was not merely theological - it was political. The Crown determined acceptable doctrine, enforced conformity, and punished deviation. Dissenters were fined, imprisoned, exiled, or worse. Belief was not treated as conscience, but as loyalty. To worship incorrectly was to threaten the state.

Speech and press followed the same logic. Printing required licenses. Unauthorized publications were suppressed. Criticism of authority was treated as sedition. Truth was not a defense. What mattered was whether speech undermined order or questioned legitimacy. Assemblies were restricted not because they were violent, but because they were collective. Petitioning authority was tolerated only when deferential.

These practices crossed the Atlantic intact. Several colonies maintained established churches. Taxes supported clergy. Office-holding was conditioned on religious tests. Dissenting ministers were jailed. Printers were prosecuted. Public meetings were monitored. None of this was considered extraordinary. It was governance as understood.

Even revolutionary governments were not immune. Once independence was declared, states experimented with regulating speech to maintain unity, suppressing criticism in the name of survival. The impulse to manage thought did not disappear with the Crown. It merely changed hands.

Why This Abuse Was Inevitable

Control of belief and expression is among the most efficient forms of power.

Belief shapes loyalty. Speech spreads doubt. Assemblies generate alternatives. Left unchecked, authority gravitates toward regulating all three - often with sincere justification. Leaders convince themselves that unity is necessary, that dissent is dangerous, and that stability requires guidance.

Religious establishment promises moral order. Speech regulation promises civility. Press control promises truth. Assembly limits promise safety. Petition restrictions promise efficiency. Each claim is defensible in isolation. Together, they form a comprehensive system of managed thought.

History shows that governments rarely begin by banning ideas outright. They license. They regulate. They prioritize approved voices. They discourage "harmful" expression. They define acceptable belief. Over time, permission replaces freedom.

The inevitability lies not in malice, but in incentive. Power benefits from conformity. Dissent complicates administration. Independent thought resists coordination. The First Amendment exists because these pressures recur regardless of intent.

What the Amendment Actually Restrains

The First Amendment restrains Congress - not citizens, not churches, not private institutions. It denies the federal government authority in five related areas:

Establishment of religion - the power to declare, support, or privilege an official belief system

12

The Bill of Rights

Free exercise of religion - the power to compel or prohibit sincere religious practice

Freedom of speech - the power to punish expression based on content or viewpoint

Freedom of the press - the power to license, censor, or suppress publication

Assembly and petition - the power to prevent collective dissent or grievances

The amendment does not guarantee harmony, truth, civility, or correctness. It does not promise protection from offense. It does not require government neutrality of outcome. It forbids government control of conscience and expression.

Its purpose is not to elevate speech, but to limit authority.

How This Right Is Commonly Misunderstood

The First Amendment is often treated as a moral endorsement rather than a legal restraint.

Religious freedom is reframed as freedom from religion rather than freedom of conscience. Speech is protected selectively based on perceived value. Press freedom is conflated with institutional credibility. Assembly is tolerated only when orderly. Petition is respected only when symbolic.

Most critically, the amendment is invoked to shape society rather than to restrain government. This reverses its function. The First Amendment does not exist to curate culture. It exists to prevent centralized control of belief and expression.

When offense becomes justification, regulation follows. When harmony becomes the goal, dissent becomes suspect. When truth is administered, error becomes punishable. These are not new developments. They are the same abuses, described in modern language.

What Happens When the Memory Fades

When the historical abuses are forgotten, the protections feel excessive.

The Bill of Rights

Speech becomes dangerous. Belief becomes inconvenient. Assemblies become disruptions. Petitions become noise. Gradually, permission replaces right. Exceptions accumulate. Enforcement becomes uneven. Authority expands without announcement.

What once restrained government becomes something government manages. The transition is rarely dramatic. It is procedural. It is justified. It is always temporary - until it is not.

The First Amendment fails not when it is repealed, but when it is reinterpreted as optional.

CHAPTER CONCLUSION

The First Amendment was written because belief, speech, and association had already been controlled - repeatedly, deliberately, and with confidence in their necessity.

It assumes that authority will seek to manage thought, not because it is tyrannical, but because it is efficient. It denies government the tools that history showed were most easily abused. It does not promise virtue. It prevents compulsion.

When the right is remembered as a protection against specific historical practices, it remains essential. When it is treated as an abstract ideal, it becomes negotiable.

The First Amendment endures not because it is inspirational, but because it is suspicious - and because history taught that suspicion was warranted.

The Bill of Rights

CHAPTER 2 – The Second Amendment

THE SECOND AMENDMENT
Preventing the Monopoly of Force

This amendment responds to a recurring historical pattern in which governments consolidate coercive power by disarming those they govern. It reflects the understanding that liberty cannot endure where force is held exclusively by authority.

The Text of the Amendment
A well regulated Militia, being necessary to the security of a free State, the right of the people to keep and bear Arms, shall not be infringed.

The Abuse That Preceded It
The Second Amendment addresses a recurring historical reality: the consolidation of force in the hands of the state.

In English history, disarmament was a political tool. Arms ownership was restricted by class, loyalty, and favor. Governments did not seek to eliminate weapons universally; they sought to control who possessed them. Those deemed trustworthy were armed. Those deemed suspect were not. Disarmament followed dissent.

Standing armies were another source of fear. Kings maintained professional forces loyal to the Crown rather than the people. These armies enforced policy, suppressed unrest, collected taxes, and maintained order. Civil authority blurred into military power. Resistance became rebellion by definition.

Colonial experience reinforced these fears. British attempts to seize colonial arms were not symbolic - they were strategic. Disarmament preceded enforcement. Lexington and Concord were not about hunting tools; they were about the control of force. Colonists understood that once arms were surrendered, resistance ceased to be possible.

The Bill of Rights

Even after independence, Americans remained wary. A centralized army, controlled by a distant authority, resembled the very system they had resisted. The fear was not invasion, but internal coercion.

Why This Abuse Was Inevitable

Force is the foundation of authority.

Law without enforcement is suggestion. Enforcement requires coercive capacity. Over time, governments seek reliability, efficiency, and control in enforcement. This naturally favors centralized, professional forces. Independent armed populations complicate administration. They resist uniformity. They limit leverage.

From the perspective of authority, disarmament appears reasonable. It reduces risk. It simplifies control. It prevents rebellion. Each justification sounds responsible. Each ignores the historical lesson that concentrated force invites abuse.

The inevitability lies in incentive. Governments prefer to hold power exclusively. Shared force is unpredictable. Distributed capability limits command. The Second Amendment exists because history showed that once force is monopolized, restraint becomes optional.

What the Amendment Actually Restrains

The Second Amendment restrains the federal government from disarming the people.

It does not grant the right to bear arms; it recognizes that the right already exists. It ties that right to the security of a free state, not to recreation, profession, or sport. The militia referenced is not a standing army. It is the people themselves, capable of defense.

The amendment denies government the authority to render the population dependent on state protection alone. It preserves a balance - not to encourage violence, but to prevent domination.

The focus is structural, not individualistic. Arms ownership functions as a political safeguard, not merely a personal preference.

The Bill of Rights

How This Right Is Commonly Misunderstood

The Second Amendment is often reduced to modern utility or dismissed as outdated.

Debates focus on technology, crime, or intent, while ignoring the historical purpose. The amendment is treated as a cultural artifact rather than a political restraint. Its language is parsed as inconvenience rather than warning.

Equally common is the belief that force can be safely centralized if intentions are good or oversight exists. History contradicts this confidence. Oversight erodes. Intent changes. Authority expands. The same tools used for protection become tools of enforcement.

When the Second Amendment is discussed only in terms of personal use, its structural role disappears.

What Happens When the Memory Fades

When the history is forgotten, disarmament becomes administrative.

Licensing expands. Exceptions narrow. Authority decides who may possess force and under what conditions. The people become subjects protected by permission rather than participants in security.

The transition is gradual. It is framed as safety. It is justified as modernization. By the time dependency is complete, resistance is no longer possible - by design.

The Second Amendment does not fail because weapons disappear. It fails because balance disappears.

CHAPTER CONCLUSION

The Second Amendment was written because power consistently sought to monopolize force, and history showed that such monopolies rarely restrained themselves.

It assumes that authority, once armed exclusively, will eventually enforce its will without meaningful opposition. It preserves a counterweight not to provoke conflict, but to prevent submission.

The Bill of Rights

When remembered as a response to real historical practices, the amendment remains intelligible. When reduced to preference or fear, its purpose is lost.

The right to bear arms was not written to enable violence. It was written to prevent the inevitability of control.

The Bill of Rights

CHAPTER 3 – The Third Amendment

THE THIRD AMENDMENT
Preventing Domestic Military Occupation

This amendment addresses the collapse of the boundary between civilian life and military authority. It exists because history showed that liberty erodes rapidly when armed power is embedded within private life.

The Text of the Amendment
No Soldier shall, in time of peace be quartered in any house, without the consent of the Owner, nor in time of war, but in a manner to be prescribed by law.

The Abuse That Preceded It
The Third Amendment responds to a form of intrusion that is rarely discussed today precisely because it was once common.

Under British rule, quartering soldiers in private homes was a standard practice. Civilians were expected to house, feed, and accommodate troops stationed among them. This was not presented as punishment, but as necessity. Armies needed shelter. The population was expected to provide it.

In the American colonies, the practice became deeply resented. British troops were stationed not as defenders against foreign threats, but as enforcers of imperial policy. Their presence was constant, intimate, and coercive. Homes ceased to be private spaces. Families lived under surveillance. Property was repurposed without consent.

The Quartering Acts formalized this arrangement. Colonists were legally compelled to support occupying forces. Refusal invited penalties. Compliance bred resentment. The line between civilian life and military authority dissolved.

The Bill of Rights

What made the abuse especially galling was its symbolism. A soldier in the home represented more than inconvenience. It was a declaration that military power superseded civil authority and personal sovereignty.

Why This Abuse Was Inevitable

Armies seek proximity to control.

Stationing troops among civilians offers advantages. It deters resistance. It shortens response time. It normalizes military presence. From the perspective of authority, quartering is efficient. It embeds power where compliance is expected.

The abuse becomes inevitable when military necessity is allowed to override civilian boundaries. Once the home is treated as a public resource, nothing remains private. Consent becomes irrelevant. Law follows convenience.

History shows that occupying forces rarely view civilians as equals. Proximity breeds dominance, not partnership. The Third Amendment exists because the Founders understood that liberty cannot survive when the military lives inside the home.

What the Amendment Actually Restrains

The Third Amendment restrains the federal government from using private homes as military infrastructure.

It establishes a clear boundary between civilian life and military authority. Even in wartime, quartering must follow law, not discretion. In peacetime, it requires consent.

The amendment does not concern comfort. It concerns sovereignty. The home is treated as an extension of the person, not a convenience of the state. By denying military occupation, the amendment preserves the distinction between civil governance and armed enforcement.

How This Right Is Commonly Misunderstood

The Third Amendment is often dismissed as obsolete.

Because modern armies rarely quarter soldiers in private homes, the amendment is viewed as a historical curiosity. Its deeper principle - that the

The Bill of Rights

military must remain subordinate and separate from civilian life - is overlooked.

This misunderstanding narrows the amendment to its literal wording rather than its intent. The danger it addresses is not housing soldiers. It is the normalization of armed authority within private life.

What Happens When the Memory Fades

When the principle is forgotten, military and police power drift inward.

Surveillance expands. Enforcement embeds itself in daily life. The distinction between civilian space and state authority weakens. While the form changes, the effect remains: privacy erodes, and coercion becomes familiar.

The Third Amendment fades quietly because its violation rarely announces itself. It appears as necessity. It appears as protection. It appears as temporary.

CHAPTER CONCLUSION

The Third Amendment was written because civilians had already experienced life under domestic military presence, and it was incompatible with liberty.

It assumes that armed authority, once welcomed into the home, does not easily leave. It draws a hard boundary where history showed none would otherwise exist.

The amendment endures not because soldiers still seek quarters, but because power still seeks proximity. Liberty requires distance.

The Bill of Rights

CHAPTER 4 – The Fourth Amendment

THE FOURTH AMENDMENT
Preventing Arbitrary Search and Surveillance

This amendment responds to the use of investigation as a tool of control rather than justice. It reflects the recognition that liberty cannot survive where intrusion requires no justification.

The Text of the Amendment
The right of the people to be secure in their persons, houses, papers, and effects, against unreasonable searches and seizures, shall not be violated, and no Warrants shall issue, but upon probable cause, supported by Oath or affirmation, and particularly describing the place to be searched, and the persons or things to be seized.

The Abuse That Preceded It
The Fourth Amendment arose directly from the experience of arbitrary search.

In England, general warrants authorized officials to search homes and seize property without naming a specific person or place. These warrants were broad, open-ended, and discretionary. They did not require individualized suspicion. Authority searched first and justified later.

In the American colonies, writs of assistance extended this practice. Customs officers could enter homes, businesses, and ships in search of contraband. Refusal was unlawful. Compliance was mandatory. The power was not targeted; it was ambient.

These searches were not rare. They were routine. Entire neighborhoods could be subjected to inspection. Private papers were examined. Property was seized. Innocence offered no protection. The burden rested entirely on the citizen.

The Bill of Rights

What made these practices especially corrosive was their invisibility. There was no public trial, no accusation, no defense. Search itself became punishment. Surveillance replaced suspicion.

Why This Abuse Was Inevitable

Investigation favors convenience.

When authority is tasked with enforcement, it seeks the path of least resistance. Broad search powers reduce effort. They increase results. They allow fishing rather than proving. From an administrative perspective, general warrants are efficient.

The temptation is constant. If wrongdoing might exist, why require proof before intrusion? If safety is at stake, why tolerate uncertainty? If enforcement is justified, why restrict method?

History shows that once granted, such powers expand. Targets broaden. Standards loosen. Oversight fades. Surveillance becomes normalized. The Fourth Amendment exists because unchecked search authority inevitably turns from protection to control.

What the Amendment Actually Restrains

The Fourth Amendment restrains the government's power to intrude.

It does not prohibit all searches. It prohibits unreasonable ones. It requires specificity, accountability, and cause. Authority must justify intrusion before it occurs, not after. The amendment reverses the presumption of access.

By protecting persons, homes, papers, and effects, it defines privacy as a condition of liberty. Security is not a privilege granted by compliance. It is a right retained absent cause.

How This Right Is Commonly Misunderstood

The Fourth Amendment is often framed as a technical obstacle.

Search protections are treated as loopholes. Warrants are viewed as formalities. Privacy is described as concealment rather than dignity. The right is tolerated when convenient and bypassed when urgent.

The Bill of Rights

Modern technology compounds this misunderstanding. Surveillance becomes passive. Data replaces doors. Search occurs without presence. Intrusion becomes invisible. The language of the amendment feels antiquated while its purpose becomes more urgent.

When privacy is reduced to secrecy, the principle is lost.

What Happens When the Memory Fades

When the historical abuse is forgotten, intrusion feels justified.

Data is collected broadly. Searches become predictive. Suspicion shifts from individualized to statistical. Authority gains access first and evaluates later. Citizens adjust behavior accordingly.

The erosion is subtle. There is no single violation. There is accumulation. Over time, security is no longer something people possess. It is something they are allowed.

CHAPTER CONCLUSION

The Fourth Amendment was written because search power had already been abused, and because unchecked investigation proved incompatible with liberty.

It assumes that authority will seek access unless restrained. It denies government the ability to intrude without justification. It preserves privacy not to shield wrongdoing, but to protect dignity.

When remembered as a response to real historical practices, the amendment remains clear. When treated as inconvenience, it erodes.

Liberty cannot survive where intrusion requires no reason.

The Bill of Rights

CHAPTER 5 – The Fifth Amendment

THE FIFTH AMENDMENT
Preventing Forced Confession and Legal Abuse

This amendment addresses the transformation of law from restraint into weapon. It exists because history showed that, without firm limits, legal process itself becomes a means of coercion.

The Text of the Amendment
No person shall be held to answer for a capital, or otherwise infamous crime, unless on a presentment or indictment of a Grand Jury, except in cases arising in the land or naval forces, or in the Militia, when in actual service in time of War or public danger; nor shall any person be subject for the same offence to be twice put in jeopardy of life or limb; nor shall be compelled in any criminal case to be a witness against himself, nor be deprived of life, liberty, or property, without due process of law; nor shall private property be taken for public use, without just compensation.

The Abuse That Preceded It
The Fifth Amendment responds to some of the oldest and most corrosive abuses of legal power.

In England, courts such as the Star Chamber and High Commission operated without juries, relied on compelled testimony, and punished silence as guilt. Confession was not evidence discovered; it was evidence extracted. The accused bore the burden of proving innocence, often under threat, coercion, or imprisonment.

Double jeopardy was another tool of pressure. Authorities could retry individuals repeatedly until conviction was achieved. Acquittal did not end prosecution. The process itself became punishment.

Property seizure followed similar logic. Assets were taken through fines, forfeitures, or royal prerogative. Compensation was optional. Due process yielded to expediency. Legal procedure became a means of control rather than a restraint on power.

Colonial governments inherited these practices. While abuses were sometimes moderated, the underlying assumptions remained. Law existed to serve authority first, justice second.

Why This Abuse Was Inevitable

Confession simplifies enforcement.

Compelled testimony eliminates uncertainty. It shortens investigation. It transfers the burden of proof to the accused. From the perspective of authority, it is efficient and decisive.

Similarly, repeated prosecution increases the likelihood of conviction. Property seizure funds enforcement. Due process slows outcomes. Each safeguard introduces friction. Power naturally seeks to remove friction.

The inevitability lies in incentive. When outcomes matter more than process, restraint erodes. Legal systems drift toward results-based justice. The Fifth Amendment exists because history showed that without firm limits, law becomes coercive.

What the Amendment Actually Restrains

The Fifth Amendment restrains the government's ability to extract, retry, deprive, and seize.

It denies the power to compel self-incrimination. It denies the power to prosecute repeatedly. It denies the power to punish without procedure. It denies the power to take property without compensation.

These protections are not expressions of sympathy for the guilty. They are acknowledgments of human vulnerability under authority. The amendment shifts the burden of proof entirely onto the state.

Due process is not efficiency. It is restraint.

How This Right Is Commonly Misunderstood

The Fifth Amendment is often portrayed as a refuge for the guilty.

The Bill of Rights

Silence is framed as evasion. Procedure is framed as obstruction. Compensation is framed as inconvenience. The safeguards are treated as technicalities rather than boundaries.

In practice, this misunderstanding invites erosion. Exceptions multiply. Emergencies justify shortcuts. Over time, compulsion reenters under new language - cooperation, compliance, administrative necessity.

When process is treated as expendable, justice becomes conditional.

What Happens When the Memory Fades

When historical abuses are forgotten, coercion becomes subtle.

Confession is encouraged rather than compelled. Prosecution is layered. Property is seized provisionally. Due process is delayed. Each step appears reasonable. Together, they reconstruct the very system the amendment was designed to prevent.

The law remains intact in form while hollowed in practice.

CHAPTER CONCLUSION

The Fifth Amendment was written because law had already been used as a weapon rather than a shield.

It assumes that authority will seek confession, conviction, and control unless restrained. It places burden, cost, and risk squarely on the state. It protects the individual not by trust, but by structure.

When remembered as a response to specific historical abuses, the amendment retains its force. When treated as a technical nuisance, coercion returns.

Justice requires limits, not efficiency.

The Bill of Rights

CHAPTER 6 – The Sixth Amendment

THE SIXTH AMENDMENT
Preventing Secret Justice

This amendment responds to systems of prosecution designed for advantage rather than fairness. It reflects the understanding that justice loses legitimacy when it operates beyond public view and meaningful challenge.

The Text of the Amendment
In all criminal prosecutions, the accused shall enjoy the right to a speedy and public trial, by an impartial jury of the State and district wherein the crime shall have been committed, which district shall have been previously ascertained by law, and to be informed of the nature and cause of the accusation; to be confronted with the witnesses against him; to have compulsory process for obtaining witnesses in his favor, and to have the Assistance of Counsel for his defence.

The Abuse That Preceded It
The Sixth Amendment was written in response to systems of justice that operated in secrecy, delay, and imbalance.

In England, trials could be delayed indefinitely. Accused individuals were held without timely resolution. Imprisonment itself became punishment regardless of outcome. Proceedings were often opaque. Accusations were vague. Evidence could be concealed. Witnesses could testify anonymously or without confrontation.

Juries, when used, were not always impartial. Venue could be manipulated to favor authority. Defendants were frequently denied legal representation, expected to defend themselves against trained prosecutors and the machinery of the state.

Colonial experience reflected these patterns. Distance, delay, and procedural imbalance favored the government. Justice was not denied outright; it was deferred, obscured, and controlled.

The Bill of Rights

The danger was not merely wrongful conviction. It was the transformation of justice into a process citizens could not observe, understand, or challenge.

Why This Abuse Was Inevitable

Secrecy favors authority.

Public trials expose weakness. Speed creates accountability. Confrontation invites challenge. Counsel equalizes power. Each safeguard complicates prosecution. From the perspective of enforcement, these are obstacles.

Authority benefits from delay. Time exhausts the accused. It weakens defense. It pressures settlement or confession. Closed proceedings reduce scrutiny. Controlled venues improve outcomes.

The inevitability lies in imbalance. When one party controls accusation, evidence, timing, and procedure, justice becomes administrative rather than adversarial. The Sixth Amendment exists because history showed that fairness does not survive convenience.

What the Amendment Actually Restrains

The Sixth Amendment restrains the government's control over criminal prosecution.

It requires speed, transparency, and locality. It demands notice, confrontation, and balance. It denies the state the ability to prosecute in secret, delay resolution indefinitely, or overwhelm the accused through procedural advantage.

The amendment does not guarantee acquittal. It guarantees exposure. Justice must be visible to be legitimate.

How This Right Is Commonly Misunderstood

The Sixth Amendment is often reduced to courtroom formality.

Speedy trials are treated as negotiable. Public proceedings are limited by administrative concerns. Jury impartiality is assumed rather than ensured. Counsel is minimized.

The Bill of Rights

Most dangerously, efficiency is allowed to replace fairness. Resolution becomes the goal. Due process becomes a hurdle. The adversarial system softens into managed outcome.

When justice is no longer seen, trust erodes.

What Happens When the Memory Fades

When the history is forgotten, prosecution becomes procedural.

Cases drag on. Detention replaces adjudication. Accusations remain vague. Defense is constrained. Trials occur, but legitimacy fades.

The system still functions. Convictions still occur. But justice becomes something done to the accused, not something done in public.

CHAPTER CONCLUSION

The Sixth Amendment was written because secret, delayed, and imbalanced justice had already proven abusive.

It assumes that authority will seek advantage unless restrained. It forces exposure, balance, and accountability. It treats visibility as protection.

When remembered as a response to real historical practices, the amendment remains essential. When treated as procedural noise, injustice returns quietly.

Justice that cannot be seen cannot be trusted.

The Bill of Rights

CHAPTER 7 – The Seventh Amendment

THE SEVENTH AMENDMENT
Preventing the Elimination of Civil Redress

This amendment addresses the quiet removal of ordinary people from the administration of civil justice. It exists because liberty erodes not only through criminal punishment, but through loss of participation in ordinary disputes.

The Text of the Amendment
In Suits at common law, where the value in controversy shall exceed twenty dollars, the right of trial by jury shall be preserved, and no fact tried by a jury, shall be otherwise re-examined in any Court of the United States, than according to the rules of the common law.

The Abuse That Preceded It
The Seventh Amendment responds to a quieter but equally consequential abuse: the removal of ordinary citizens from civil justice.

In English history, civil disputes were increasingly absorbed by royal courts and administrative bodies. Juries were bypassed in favor of judges aligned with the Crown. Outcomes became predictable. Remedies favored authority, merchants with influence, or the state itself. Ordinary litigants faced systems they could not meaningfully challenge.

Civil cases were not trivial. Property rights, contracts, debts, and personal injury determined livelihoods and survival. When these disputes were decided exclusively by officials rather than peers, justice shifted from communal judgment to administrative convenience.

Colonial courts replicated this structure. Governors and appointed judges exercised broad discretion. Juries were sometimes restricted, overridden, or avoided altogether. The loss was not dramatic. It was procedural. Citizens slowly ceased to be participants in justice and became subjects of it.

The Bill of Rights

Why This Abuse Was Inevitable
Administration prefers predictability.

Juries are inefficient. They are unpredictable. They introduce community values into legal outcomes. From the perspective of authority, juries complicate enforcement and policy consistency.

Civil disputes offer particular temptation. They involve money rather than liberty. The stakes appear lower. The public pays less attention. Yet control of civil justice determines economic power, property ownership, and long-term stability.

The inevitability lies in control. When authority decides facts, it shapes outcomes. When outcomes matter, authority seeks to decide facts. The Seventh Amendment exists because history showed that civil justice drifts toward consolidation unless restrained.

What the Amendment Actually Restrains
The Seventh Amendment restrains the federal government from eliminating juries in civil cases.

It preserves the role of ordinary citizens in resolving disputes of fact. It limits judicial re-examination. It prevents the quiet absorption of civil justice into bureaucratic systems.

The amendment does not guarantee favorable verdicts. It guarantees participation. Civil liberty depends not only on protection from prison, but on protection from dispossession.

How This Right Is Commonly Misunderstood
The Seventh Amendment is often dismissed as technical or obsolete.

Civil juries are portrayed as costly, slow, or unsophisticated. Administrative adjudication is framed as progress. Expertise replaces judgment. Efficiency replaces fairness.

Because civil cases lack the drama of criminal trials, erosion goes unnoticed. Rights disappear through procedure rather than decree.

The Bill of Rights

When citizens are removed from civil justice, accountability follows.

What Happens When the Memory Fades

When the historical abuse is forgotten, civil justice becomes managed.

Disputes are resolved internally. Appeals are limited. Standards shift. Citizens encounter systems designed for throughput rather than fairness.

Property changes hands. Contracts are enforced selectively. Remedies favor institutions. The loss is cumulative.

Justice still exists, but it no longer belongs to the people.

CHAPTER CONCLUSION

The Seventh Amendment was written because civil justice had already been centralized, professionalized, and removed from public judgment.

It assumes that authority prefers predictability to participation. It preserves the jury not as tradition, but as restraint.

Liberty is not threatened only by prison cells. It is threatened when ordinary people no longer decide ordinary disputes.

When civil justice becomes administrative, freedom becomes conditional.

The Bill of Rights

CHAPTER 8 – The Eighth Amendment

THE EIGHTH AMENDMENT
Preventing Punishment as Deterrent Theater

This amendment responds to the historic use of punishment as spectacle and intimidation. It reflects the recognition that severity, once untethered from restraint, becomes a tool of domination rather than justice.

The Text of the Amendment
Excessive bail shall not be required, nor excessive fines imposed, nor cruel and unusual punishments inflicted.

The Abuse That Preceded It
The Eighth Amendment responds to the historic use of punishment not merely to correct wrongdoing, but to display power.

In England and across Europe, punishment was often public, theatrical, and deliberately severe. Executions were spectacles. Mutilation, branding, whipping, and prolonged suffering were designed to instruct the population through fear. Justice was not only imposed; it was performed.

Excessive bail served a similar purpose. It detained the accused before trial, ensuring punishment regardless of guilt. Fines were used not only as penalties, but as revenue. They scaled not to offense, but to advantage. Punishment became a tool of control rather than correction.

Colonial governments inherited these practices. While the most extreme forms diminished over time, the underlying logic persisted: punishment deters best when it is visible, severe, and exemplary.

The abuse was not excess alone. It was intentional excess.

Why This Abuse Was Inevitable
Fear is an efficient motivator.

The Bill of Rights

Severe punishment simplifies enforcement. It reduces resistance. It discourages dissent. From the perspective of authority, harshness appears effective.

Bail can incapacitate before conviction. Fines can fund enforcement. Cruelty signals seriousness. Each tool strengthens control while bypassing the complexity of proportional justice.

The inevitability lies in demonstration. Authority seeks not only compliance, but submission. When punishment becomes symbolic, restraint disappears. The Eighth Amendment exists because history showed that punishment, once unbounded, becomes spectacle.

What the Amendment Actually Restrains

The Eighth Amendment restrains the government's power to punish excessively.

It does not eliminate punishment. It limits severity. It requires proportionality. It denies the state the authority to punish for display, revenue, or intimidation.

The amendment recognizes that punishment can be abused even after guilt is established. Justice does not end at conviction. Power must remain restrained at every stage.

How This Right Is Commonly Misunderstood

The Eighth Amendment is often interpreted narrowly.

Cruelty is defined only as physical pain. Excessiveness is reduced to arithmetic. Bail is treated as procedural. Fines are justified as deterrents without regard to impact.

This misunderstanding allows punishment to escalate in form while appearing lawful. Severity shifts from physical to financial, from public spectacle to systemic burden.

When punishment is measured only by legality, abuse returns.

The Bill of Rights

What Happens When the Memory Fades

When the history is forgotten, punishment becomes strategic.

Bail ensures detention. Fines generate revenue. Conditions degrade. Deterrence replaces rehabilitation. The system remains orderly, but dignity erodes.

Fear returns quietly, enforced through policy rather than spectacle.

CHAPTER CONCLUSION

The Eighth Amendment was written because punishment had already been used as a tool of domination rather than justice.

It assumes that authority will push severity unless restrained. It denies the state the ability to punish for effect. It insists that justice retain humanity.

When remembered as a response to historical cruelty, the amendment remains clear. When treated as outdated sentiment, excess returns.

Punishment that serves power rather than justice corrupts both.

The Bill of Rights

CHAPTER 9 – The Ninth Amendment

THE NINTH AMENDMENT
Preventing the Claim That Rights Are Exhaustive

This amendment addresses the danger created by written enumeration itself. It exists because history showed that silence, when treated as surrender, becomes a powerful instrument of control.

The Text of the Amendment
The enumeration in the Constitution, of certain rights, shall not be construed to deny or disparage others retained by the people.

The Abuse That Preceded It
The Ninth Amendment responds to a subtler danger than open coercion: the abuse of silence.

Throughout legal history, authority repeatedly exploited what was not written. Powers were claimed not because they were granted, but because they were not explicitly denied. Rights were dismissed not because they were illegitimate, but because they were undefined.

English common law offered some protections, but only so long as authority acknowledged them. When convenient, silence was reinterpreted as permission. What could not be pointed to in text could be ignored in practice.

This danger intensified with written constitutions. Once rights began to be listed, a new risk emerged: that enumeration itself would become limitation. What was named would be protected. What was unlisted would be treated as surrendered.

Several framers recognized this immediately. They feared that a bill of rights, however well intentioned, might be turned against the people - used to argue that liberty exists only where specified.

The Ninth Amendment exists because that concern was not hypothetical. It was historically grounded.

The Bill of Rights

Law favors clarity, but power favors closure.

Once authority operates through text, it seeks completeness. Enumerated lists invite interpretation as boundaries. What lies outside the list appears excluded.

From the perspective of governance, this is efficient. It simplifies adjudication. It limits uncertainty. It confines claims. Over time, rights shrink not by repeal, but by omission.

The inevitability lies in legal logic. If rights are treated as grants rather than possessions, silence becomes surrender. The Ninth Amendment exists because history showed that enumeration without humility invites control.

What the Amendment Actually Restrains

The Ninth Amendment restrains interpretive authority.

It denies the government the power to claim that rights exist only where listed. It affirms that the people retain liberties beyond those enumerated. It preserves the distinction between recognition and creation.

The amendment does not define additional rights. It forbids denial by inference. It functions as a guardrail against textual absolutism.

Its purpose is not expansion. It is prevention.

How This Right Is Commonly Misunderstood

The Ninth Amendment is often treated as vague or decorative.

Because it does not list rights or prescribe enforcement, it is dismissed as nonfunctional. In practice, it is ignored. Silence is allowed to operate as exclusion.

This misunderstanding transforms the Constitution into a permission structure rather than a restraint. Rights become claims that must be proven rather than liberties that must be respected.

When the Ninth Amendment is neglected, enumeration becomes enclosure.

The Bill of Rights

What Happens When the Memory Fades

When the historical concern is forgotten, rights contract.

Authority asks not whether it may infringe, but whether it is forbidden. If prohibition cannot be found, action proceeds. Liberty erodes through interpretation rather than decree.

The Constitution remains intact. The language remains unchanged. Only the scope of retained rights narrows.

CHAPTER CONCLUSION

The Ninth Amendment was written because the framers understood that written protections carry inherent risk.

It assumes that authority will treat silence as surrender unless restrained. It preserves liberty beyond text. It acknowledges that no document can capture the full scope of human freedom.

When remembered, the Ninth Amendment humbles interpretation. When forgotten, it enables enclosure.

Rights that exist only by enumeration are not rights at all.

The Bill of Rights

CHAPTER 10 – The Tenth Amendment

THE TENTH AMENDMENT
Preventing Total Consolidation

This amendment responds to the steady accumulation of authority through interpretation and convenience. It reflects the understanding that power consolidates not by force alone, but by default.

The Text of the Amendment
The powers not delegated to the United States by the Constitution, nor prohibited by it to the States, are reserved to the States respectively, or to the people.

The Abuse That Preceded It
The Tenth Amendment responds to the oldest political failure: the gradual consolidation of power.

In English history, authority accumulated steadily in the Crown. Local customs, regional autonomy, and traditional liberties were absorbed into centralized administration. Power did not seize all at once. It gathered incrementally, justified by necessity, efficiency, or uniformity.

Colonial governments experienced similar patterns. Governors appointed from afar exercised authority over distant populations. Local governance existed at the pleasure of centralized power. Appeals traveled upward. Control flowed downward.

Even during the formation of the United States, this danger was recognized. The new federal government, though limited in design, possessed the potential to expand. Ambiguous authority invites interpretation. Interpretation invites consolidation.

The Tenth Amendment exists because the framers knew that structure alone would not hold without reaffirmation.

The Bill of Rights

Why This Abuse Was Inevitable

Power seeks coherence.

Fragmented authority frustrates administration. Local variation complicates enforcement. Centralization promises clarity, uniformity, and control. From the perspective of authority, consolidation appears rational.

Over time, functions migrate upward. Exceptions harden into precedent. Temporary measures persist. What begins as coordination becomes command.

The inevitability lies in scope. Without explicit reservation, power fills vacuum. The Tenth Amendment exists because absence of denial becomes invitation.

What the Amendment Actually Restrains

The Tenth Amendment restrains federal overreach.

It affirms that the federal government possesses only delegated powers. All others remain with the states or the people. It denies the presumption of comprehensive authority.

This amendment does not enumerate powers. It denies expansion by inference. It reinforces the principle that sovereignty flows upward, not downward.

It is structural, not symbolic.

How This Right Is Commonly Misunderstood

The Tenth Amendment is often dismissed as redundant.

Because powers are enumerated elsewhere, the amendment is treated as reminder rather than restraint. Its enforcement is viewed as political rather than constitutional.

This misunderstanding allows consolidation to proceed under interpretation. Federal authority expands not by amendment, but by assumption. States become administrators. Citizens become subjects of unified policy.

The Bill of Rights

When reservation is ignored, consolidation accelerates.

What Happens When the Memory Fades

When the historical danger is forgotten, centralization becomes normal.

Local authority erodes. Uniform standards replace contextual judgment. Policy flows from distance. Accountability diffuses.

The Constitution remains intact. Power shifts anyway.

CHAPTER CONCLUSION

The Tenth Amendment was written because the framers understood that consolidation does not require conquest.

It assumes that authority will expand unless restrained. It preserves division as protection. It anchors sovereignty where proximity ensures accountability.

When remembered, the Tenth Amendment stabilizes the entire constitutional structure. When forgotten, every other right weakens.

Liberty survives not through concentration, but through restraint.

and a final conclusion?

The Bill of Rights

CONCLUSION

When Memory Fails, Power Returns

The Bill of Rights was written as a response, not a declaration.

Each amendment reflects a specific abuse already experienced, already justified, and already normalized by authority. None were theoretical. None were speculative. They were drawn from memory - English memory, colonial memory, and the early memory of a nation that had learned how quickly liberty yields to convenience.

Taken together, the first ten amendments do not describe an ideal society. They describe a restrained one.

They assume that power will seek efficiency over fairness, coordination over consent, order over liberty. They assume that authority, once trusted, will eventually exceed its bounds. This assumption is not cynical. It is historical.

The Bill of Rights does not promise good governance. It prepares for failure.

Each right functions as a denial: a refusal to allow belief to be compelled, force to be monopolized, homes to be occupied, privacy to be invaded, confessions to be coerced, justice to be hidden, civil disputes to be absorbed, punishment to become spectacle, liberty to be reduced to enumeration, and power to consolidate without limit.

None of these protections require repeal to fail. They erode through reinterpretation. Memory fades. Language shifts. Exceptions multiply. What was once unthinkable becomes administratively necessary. What was once restrained becomes coordinated.

When rights are remembered as historical responses, they remain intelligible. When treated as abstract ideals, they become negotiable. The danger is not that the Bill of Rights will be rejected, but that it will be honored in name while emptied of function.

The Founders did not believe virtue would save liberty. They believed structure might. They believed memory must.

The Bill of Rights

The Bill of Rights is not a relic of distrust. It is an instruction born of experience. Its value lies not in inspiration, but in restraint.

When memory fails, power returns.

And when power returns unrestrained, history repeats - quietly, legally, and with confidence in its necessity.

The Bill of Rights

APPENDIX A

English and Colonial Abuses Referenced

The Bill of Rights did not emerge from abstract political theory alone. It was shaped by concrete practices that had already proven destructive to liberty. The following categories summarize the recurring abuses that informed the first ten amendments.

These are not exhaustive histories. They are patterns.

Compelled Religious Conformity

Governments routinely aligned political loyalty with religious adherence. Established churches received state support. Dissenters were fined, imprisoned, excluded from office, or expelled. Belief became a test of obedience rather than conscience.

This practice informed the prohibitions against establishment and compelled belief in the First Amendment.

Regulation of Speech, Press, and Assembly

Licensing regimes controlled printing. Unapproved publications were suppressed. Criticism of authority was prosecuted as sedition. Public assemblies were restricted not for violence, but for coordination. Petitioning authority was tolerated only when deferential.

These practices shaped protections for expression, press, assembly, and grievance.

Disarmament and Standing Armies

Weapons possession was restricted by class and loyalty. Populations deemed suspect were disarmed. Professional armies loyal to the Crown enforced policy internally. Military power blurred into civil authority.

These abuses informed the Second and Third Amendments.

The Bill of Rights

Quartering and Military Intrusion

Soldiers were housed among civilians without consent. Homes were treated as resources. Military presence normalized surveillance and intimidation. Civilian life became subordinate to armed authority.

This experience directly produced the Third Amendment.

General Warrants and Arbitrary Search

Authorities conducted searches without individualized suspicion. Homes, papers, and effects were examined broadly. Intrusion preceded accusation. Search itself functioned as punishment.

These practices shaped the Fourth Amendment.

Forced Confession and Star Chamber Justice

Accused individuals were compelled to testify against themselves. Silence was treated as guilt. Courts operated without juries. Outcomes favored authority. Repeated prosecution ensured conviction.

These abuses informed the Fifth and Sixth Amendments.

Secret Trials and Procedural Imbalance

Trials were delayed, hidden, or conducted without meaningful defense. Accusations were vague. Evidence was concealed. Counsel was denied. Venue was manipulated.

These conditions produced the Sixth Amendment's protections.

Administrative Civil Justice

Civil disputes were removed from juries and decided by officials aligned with power. Ordinary citizens lost participation in decisions affecting property, contracts, and livelihood.

This pattern shaped the Seventh Amendment.

Excessive Punishment and Financial Extraction

Punishment was used theatrically. Bail ensured detention. Fines funded authority. Severity replaced proportionality. Justice became deterrent display.

The Bill of Rights

These practices informed the Eighth Amendment.

Exploitation of Silence and Consolidation of Power

Unenumerated liberties were treated as nonexistent. Authority claimed powers not explicitly denied. Local autonomy eroded gradually into centralized control.

These dangers produced the Ninth and Tenth Amendments.

The Bill of Rights reflects not optimism, but memory. Each amendment corresponds to a failure already observed.

The Bill of Rights

APPENDIX B

Why a Bill of Rights Was Initially Opposed

The Bill of Rights was not universally welcomed at the founding. Its inclusion followed serious debate. Understanding these objections clarifies both the document's purpose and its limitations.

The Argument from Structure

Some framers believed a bill of rights was unnecessary because the Constitution already limited federal power. If authority was restricted to enumerated powers, additional restraints seemed redundant.

This argument assumed that structure alone would hold.

History suggested otherwise.

The Argument from Enumeration

Others feared that listing rights would invite abuse. Enumerated protections might be treated as exclusive. Unwritten liberties could be denied by omission. Silence could be reinterpreted as surrender.

This concern proved well founded and directly produced the Ninth Amendment.

The Argument from False Security

There was also concern that a bill of rights might create complacency. Citizens might trust parchment rather than vigilance. Written protections could become symbolic rather than functional.

This danger remains.

Why the Objections Were Overcome

The decision to include a Bill of Rights reflected realism rather than idealism.

Experience had shown that:

The Bill of Rights

Power expands through interpretation

Emergencies justify exceptions

Structure erodes without reinforcement

Memory fades faster than text

The Bill of Rights was adopted not because it was perfect, but because silence had proven dangerous.

What the Debate Reveals

The framers did not view the Bill of Rights as a grant of liberty. They viewed it as a set of warnings - imperfect, incomplete, but necessary.

The document carries its own caution within it.

The Bill of Rights

APPENDIX C

Rights vs Permissions

Modern misunderstandings of the Bill of Rights often arise from a failure to distinguish between rights and permissions.

This distinction is foundational.

Rights Are Retained

A right is something possessed prior to government. It exists independent of recognition. Government may acknowledge it, protect it, or violate it - but it does not create it.

The Bill of Rights assumes this posture throughout.

Permissions Are Granted

A permission is conditional. It exists at the discretion of authority. It may be expanded, restricted, revoked, or managed. Permission assumes hierarchy. Right assumes autonomy.

When rights are treated as permissions, liberty becomes contingent.

How the Shift Occurs

The shift from right to permission rarely happens openly.

It occurs through:

Licensing

Regulation

Exception

Conditional enforcement

Administrative discretion

Over time, compliance replaces possession.

The Bill of Rights

Why the Distinction Matters

Rights restrain government.
Permissions empower it.

The Bill of Rights loses force the moment its protections are treated as allowances rather than boundaries.

The Central Warning

The Constitution does not say:
"You may do these things."

It says:
"Government may not stop you from doing these things."

When that distinction is lost, the document remains intact - but liberty does not.

The Bill of Rights

AUTHOR'S NOTE

On the Chapter Conclusions

Each chapter in this book ends with a conclusion.

This is intentional.

The chapters are not essays built toward persuasion. They are examinations built toward clarity. The conclusions do not summarize arguments or propose solutions. They restore orientation.

Throughout history, rights have rarely been lost through direct rejection. They are lost through reinterpretation, neglect, and familiarity. The chapter conclusions exist to arrest drift - to restate, plainly and without embellishment, why each amendment was written and what danger it was meant to prevent.

They are not calls to action.
They are reminders of origin.

In the earlier five volumes, chapter conclusions served a similar purpose. They did not advance the narrative. They stabilized it. They provided pause in a subject that naturally accelerates toward abstraction.

The same principle applies here.

Each conclusion reinforces a single idea: that the Bill of Rights assumes inevitability, not optimism. That it restrains power because history showed restraint would otherwise fail. That its protections do not require repeal to disappear - only reinterpretation.

If these conclusions feel repetitive, that is by design. Memory requires reinforcement. Rights endure not because they are eloquent, but because their purpose is remembered.

This book does not ask the reader to agree. It asks the reader to remember.

The Bill of Rights

And remembrance, in the history of liberty, has always been the first line of defense.

END

www.ingramcontent.com/pod-product-compliance
Lightning Source LLC
Chambersburg PA
CBHW071241090426

42736CB00014B/3166